P9-DID-817

000001840084721

NORTH DAKOTA

The Peace Garden State

BY
JOHN HAMILTON

Abdo & Daughters
An imprint of Abdo Publishing | abdopublishing.com

abdopublishing.com

Published by ABDO Publishing, a division of ABDO, PO Box 398166, Minneapolis, Minnesota 55439. Copyright © 2017 by Abdo Consulting Group, Inc. International copyrights reserved in all countries. No part of this book may be reproduced in any form without written permission from the publisher. ABDO & Daughters™ is a trademark and logo of ABDO Publishing.

Printed in the United States of America, North Mankato, Minnesota.
052016
092016

THIS BOOK CONTAINS
RECYCLED MATERIALS

Editor: Sue Hamilton   **Contributing Editor:** Bridget O'Brien
Graphic Design: Sue Hamilton
Cover Art Direction: Candice Keimig   **Cover Photo Selection:** Neil Klinepier
Cover Photo: iStock
Interior Images: Alamy, AP, Brownings Honey, Corbis, David Olson, Getty Images, Fargo-Moorhead RedHawks, Fargo-Moorhead-West Fargo Chamber of Commerce, George Catlin, Glow Images, Granger, History in Full Color-Restoration/Colorization, Independence National Historical Par/C.W. Peale, iStock, John Hamilton, Karl Bodmer, Library of Congress, Mile High Maps, Minden Pictures, Mountain High Maps, North Dakota State University Bisons, One Mile Up, Science Source, State Historical Society of North Dakota, U.S. Air Force, University of North Dakota Fighting Hawks, White House, & Wikimedia.

Statistics: *State and City Populations*, U.S. Census Bureau, July 1, 2015/2014 estimates; *Land and Water Area*, U.S. Census Bureau, 2010 Census, MAF/TIGER database; *State Temperature Extremes*, NOAA National Climatic Data Center; *Climatology and Average Annual Precipitation*, NOAA National Climatic Data Center, 1980-2015 statewide averages; *State Highest and Lowest Points*, NOAA National Geodetic Survey.

Websites: To learn more about the United States, visit booklinks.abdopublishing.com. These links are routinely monitored and updated to provide the most current information available.

Cataloging-in-Publication Data
Names: Hamilton, John, 1959- author.
Title: North Dakota / by John Hamilton.
Description: Minneapolis, MN : Abdo Publishing, [2017] | Series: The United
    States of America | Includes index.
Identifiers: LCCN 2015957733 | ISBN 9781680783360 (lib. bdg.) |
    ISBN 9781680774405 (ebook)
Subjects: LCSH: North Dakota--Juvenile literature.
Classification: DDC 978.4--dc23
LC record available at http://lccn.loc.gov/2015957733

CONTENTS

THE PEACE GARDEN STATE

North Dakota is a place filled with big skies and never-ending plains. The rich soil and climate are ideal for growing vast fields of wheat and soybeans, enough to feed millions. About 89 percent of North Dakota is devoted to farming and cattle ranching. The land is dotted with grain elevators and silos, yet there are many wild places to explore.

Native Americans made their home in present-day North Dakota for thousands of years. In 1883, future president Theodore Roosevelt came to get a taste of the American frontier. "I have always said I would not have been president had it not been for my experience in North Dakota," he wrote.

The International Peace Garden straddles the border of North Dakota and Manitoba, Canada. Built in 1932, the flower-filled park is a symbol of peace between the United States and Canada. That is why North Dakota is nicknamed "The Peace Garden State."

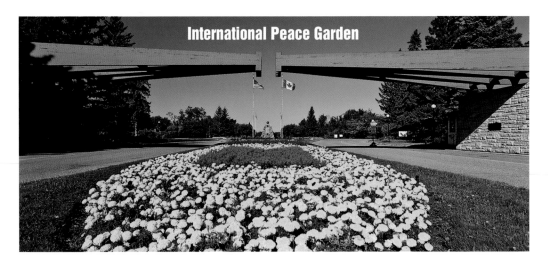

International Peace Garden

QUICK FACTS

Name: The word "Dakota" means "friend" or "ally" in the language of the Native American Sioux nation.

State Capital: Bismarck, population 68,896

Date of Statehood: November 2, 1889 (39th state)

Population: 756,927 (47th-most populous state)

Area (Total Land and Water): 70,698 square miles (183,107 sq km), 19th-largest state

Largest City: Fargo, population 115,863

Nicknames: The Peace Garden State; the Roughrider State; the Flickertail State

Motto: Liberty and Union Now and Forever, One and Inseparable

State Bird: Western Meadowlark

State Flower: Wild Prairie Rose

State Tree: American Elm

State Song: "North Dakota Hymn"

Highest Point: White Butte, 3,506 feet (1,069 m)

Lowest Point: Red River of the North, 750 feet (229 m)

Average July High Temperature: 82°F (28°C)

Record High Temperature: 121°F (49°C), in Steele on July 6, 1936

Average January Low Temperature: 1°F (-17°C)

Record Low Temperature: -60°F (-51°C), in Parshall on February 15, 1936

Average Annual Precipitation: 18 inches (46 cm)

Number of U.S. Senators: 2

Number of U.S. Representatives: 1

U.S. Postal Service Abbreviation: ND

GEOGRAPHY

North Dakota's vast plains are spread out over 70,698 square miles (183,107 sq km) of land and water. It is the 19th-largest state. It is located in the north-central part of the United States, in a region called the Great Plains. It is mostly flat, with wide areas of low, rolling hills. From east to west, the land gradually rises in elevation.

The Red River of the North marks North Dakota's eastern border with Minnesota. To the south is the state of South Dakota. To the west is Montana. Two Canadian provinces share North Dakota's northern border: Manitoba and Saskatchewan. The geographic center of North America is near the town of Rugby, North Dakota.

A stone marker in Rugby, North Dakota, shows the approximate geographic center of North America.

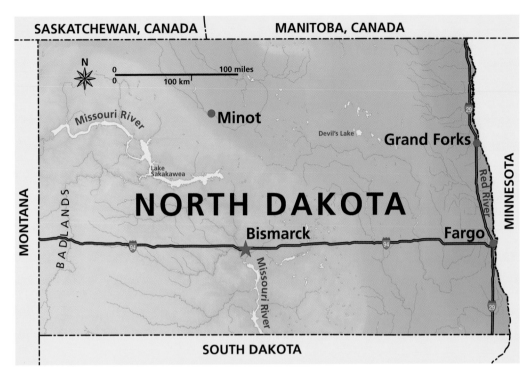

North Dakota's total land and water area
is 70,698 square miles (183,107 sq km).
It is the 19th-largest state. The state
capital is Bismarck.

The Red River Valley is in the east. It is a narrow, fertile valley that runs along the northward-flowing Red River of the North. Most of the state's people live in this region.

The Drift Prairie is a region that stretches across much of central North Dakota. Long ago, the land was covered in prairie grass. Today, most of the Drift Prairie is fertile farmland. It is mostly flat, with some gently rolling hills. There are also many small lakes and marshes—called prairie potholes—that shelter ducks, geese, and other waterfowl.

The Missouri River enters North Dakota in its northwestern corner. It flows southeast until it reaches the approximate middle of the state, then heads southward until crossing the South Dakota border. The nation's third-largest non-natural lake is a reservoir of the Missouri River. Lake Sakakawea was created in 1956 with the completion of Garrison Dam. The dam helps control floods and creates electricity. North Dakota's largest natural lake is called Devils Lake.

Cows find water in a prairie pothole.

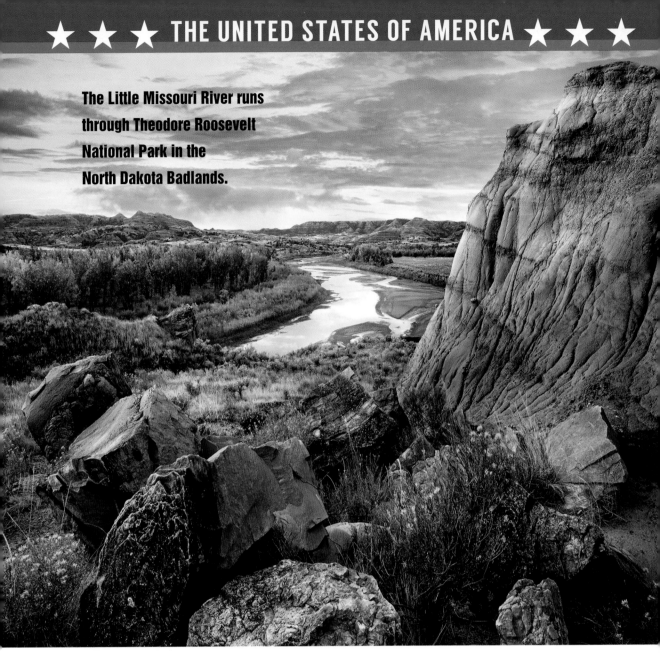

The Little Missouri River runs through Theodore Roosevelt National Park in the North Dakota Badlands.

The land south and west of the Missouri River is at a higher elevation and more arid than eastern North Dakota. Much of the land is good for growing wheat and grazing cattle and sheep.

In the far western part of North Dakota is a region called the Badlands. The clay earth is deeply eroded by wind and rain. There are high, jagged cliffs, colorful rock formations, and deep valleys. Theodore Roosevelt National Park is in the North Dakota Badlands.

CLIMATE AND
WEATHER

N orth Dakota has a continental climate, far from the moderating effects of oceans. The state experiences extremes in temperature and weather, with hot summers and very cold winters.

Summers in North Dakota can be blisteringly hot and humid. The average July high temperature is 82°F (28°C). The record high temperature occurred on July 6, 1936. On that day, the thermometer soared to 121°F (49°C) in the town of Steele.

A summer storm moves across North Dakota's Mountrail County.

A man walks through blizzard conditions in Fargo, North Dakota.

Winters can be bitterly cold. Below-zero temperatures are common. Freezing winds called Alberta Clippers often whip down from Canada. The average January low temperature is 1°F (-17°C). On February 15, 1936, in the town of Parshall, the thermometer plunged to a record low of -60°F (-51°C).

North Dakota is a dry state, but usually gets enough rain to grow crops. There is less precipitation in the western part of the state. Statewide, the average annual precipitation is 18 inches (46 cm). In winter, blizzards bring blowing wind and snow. Spring snowmelt can cause dangerous flooding, especially in the Red River Valley.

CLIMATE AND WEATHER

PLANTS AND
ANIMALS

Most of North Dakota's natural prairie has been replaced by farms. About 89 percent of the state's land area is either farmland or pasture for grazing cattle and sheep. Even though there is so much farmland, North Dakota still contains millions of acres of grasslands. The grasses provide important shelter for nesting birds and other animals. It is also good grazing land for large animals such as bison and pronghorn.

Prairie grasses have long roots, which prevent soil erosion. Some tallgrasses can reach heights of six to eight feet (1.8 to 2.4 m). Their deep roots help them survive the harsh weather conditions on the prairie. Common native North Dakota grasses include big bluestem, bluebunch, green needlegrass, buffalograss, and switchgrass. Western wheatgrass is the official state grass.

Wild horses feed on North Dakota grasses in Theodore Roosevelt National Park.

Trees line the banks of a fog-covered Little Missouri River in western North Dakota.

About one percent of North Dakota is covered by forests. Most of the wooded areas are near rivers and streams, or have been planted near farm fields to act as windbreaks. The official state tree is the American elm. It is a beautiful shade tree found near streams and lakeshores. Other common trees include ash, aspen, cottonwood, maple, walnut, and willow.

Spruce trees act as a windbreak on a North Dakota farm.

North Dakota has 63 wildlife refuges, more than any other state. Common mammals found throughout North Dakota include white-tailed deer, badgers, coyotes, long-tailed weasels, minks, eastern spotted skunks, fishers, red foxes, beavers, black-tailed prairie dogs, ground squirrels, muskrats, and raccoons. Elk and moose are found in northeastern North Dakota near the Canadian border.

Bison once thundered across the North Dakota landscape by the millions. Sadly, most were killed by overhunting. Today, small herds of bison are protected in Theodore Roosevelt National Park in western North Dakota.

Other mammals spotted in the Badlands and southwestern North Dakota include bighorn sheep, pronghorn, elk, mule deer, gray wolves, bobcats, and mountain lions.

Coyote

Pelicans

Common fish found swimming in North Dakota's many rivers and lakes include northern pike, muskellunge, walleye, perch, largemouth bass, smallmouth bass, bluegill, sunfish, crappie, channel catfish, rainbow trout, brown trout, gar, carp, and white sucker.

Hundreds of species of birds live in North Dakota. The state is along the Central Flyway. It is a route used by millions of migratory birds each spring and fall. Many species of ducks and geese are found in the state. Other common birds include white pelicans, grouse, gulls, terns, doves, red-headed woodpeckers, yellow-bellied sapsuckers, western bluebirds, wrens, red-winged blackbirds, goldfinches, loons, herons, and egrets. Raptors include osprey, bald eagles, and red-tailed hawks. The official state bird is the western meadowlark.

Prairie Rattlesnake

There are about 28 species of reptiles and amphibians in North Dakota. Prairie rattlesnakes are the state's only venomous snakes. They are found in southwestern North Dakota.

HISTORY

The first people to live in present-day North Dakota came to the area about 10,000 years ago. These Paleo-Indians were the ancient ancestors of today's Native Americans. They were nomads who hunted herds of large animals such as bison and mastodons. They eventually settled into villages. They built large earthen mounds for religious ceremonies such as burials.

By the time the first European explorers came to North Dakota in the 1500s and 1600s, several major Native American tribes had established themselves. They included the Mandan, Hidatsa, Arikara, Chippewa, and Sioux tribes.

The Mandan, Hidatsa, and Arikara people lived peacefully and farmed mainly along the Missouri River. They hunted buffalo and built earthen lodges. The Chippewa (also called the Ojibwe) and the Sioux (also called the Lakota) lived mainly on the plains. They sometimes fought rival groups for territory and to control trade. The Sioux lived in buffalo-hide tents called teepees.

In 1738, the first European arrived in North Dakota. He was French fur trader Pierre La Vérendrye. He visited several Mandan villages, and built a post to trade with the Native Americans.

French explorer Pierre La Vérendrye is the first known European to visit North Dakota.

Mah-to-toh-pa, or Four Bears, of the Mandan tribe, painted by George Catlin in 1832.

In 1803, the United States paid France $15 million for a huge piece of land called the Louisiana Purchase. (Today's state of Louisiana was just a small part of the area.) The sale almost doubled the size of the United States. Present-day North Dakota was part of the purchase.

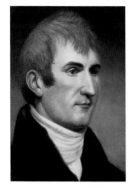

Meriwether Lewis and William Clark explored the West as leaders of the Corps of Discovery from 1804 to 1806.

President Thomas Jefferson chose Meriwether Lewis and William Clark to lead an expedition, called the Corps of Discovery, to explore the new land. In 1804, the expedition started at the mouth of the Missouri River and traveled upstream. During the winter of 1804-1805, they built a wooden fort near the present-day city of Washburn, North Dakota. They named it Fort Mandan, after the Native Americans who lived nearby.

At Fort Mandan the expedition met Sacagawea, a young Shoshone woman who later became an invaluable interpreter. In the spring, the expedition moved on, traveling all the way to the Pacific Ocean. On their return journey in 1806, they once again passed through North Dakota.

Over the next several decades, fur traders, farmers, and ranchers began to settle the land. By the 1830s, many of the Native Americans had died or been forced off their land. Diseases such as smallpox wiped out entire villages. The Native Americans had no natural immunity to the deadly infections brought by the Europeans.

On March 2, 1861, the United States government organized Dakota Territory. It included the present day states of North Dakota, South Dakota, Montana, and parts of Wyoming and Nebraska.

A reenactor stands at the entrance of a replica of Fort Mandan, built near the original site in present-day North Dakota.

In the 1880s, new railroads brought more settlers to the area. Many were immigrants from Germany, Norway, Sweden, Denmark, and Holland. They faced harsh winters, spring floods, and hot summers. However, many were successful. Large farms grew fields of profitable wheat. New towns sprang up along the railroad tracks.

On November 2, 1889, both North and South Dakota were admitted to the United States. North Dakota became the 39th state.

North Dakota's wheat and barley fields fed a hungry nation. During World War I (1914-1918), the state prospered by providing food to troops and citizens in Europe.

North Dakota farmers break soil to begin planting in the 1900s.

The Minot Air Force Base opened in 1957, bringing jobs to the area.

The economy of the United States collapsed in 1929. Millions of people lost their jobs, businesses, and homes. The Great Depression lasted for most of the 1930s. North Dakota was hit hard. In addition to the bad economy, a long drought devastated crops. Many farmers lost their land.

During World War II (1939-1945), the economy began to improve. North Dakota's wheat and other crops began selling for good prices again. In the 1950s, oil was discovered in the western part of the state. Military bases built in the 1950s further boosted the local economy by bringing jobs to North Dakota.

In recent years, North Dakota experienced rapid growth because of an oil boom. The collapse of oil prices in the mid-2010s halted much of the oil industry's growth, but many new workers have stayed in North Dakota to take advantage of the state's safe, friendly cities and beautiful landscapes.

HISTORY

DID YOU KNOW?

• Pronghorns are not really antelopes, even though they are commonly called "pronghorn antelopes." Their scientific name is *Antilocapra americana*, which means "American antelope goat." But these swift animals are neither antelope nor goat. They are part of an ancient animal species that can be traced back at least 20 million years. When the Lewis and Clark Expedition first scientifically described pronghorn, they referred to them as "antelopes" because of their resemblance to African antelopes. Pronghorns are common on the North American plains. They are among the fastest animals on Earth. They have been clocked at up to 53 miles per hour (85 kph), leaving predators such as coyotes or wolves far behind.

Pronghorn

• On November 2, 1889, President Benjamin Harrison signed two laws that divided Dakota Territory and created both North and South Dakota. But which state came first? Nobody knows for sure because President Harrison kept it a secret. He shuffled the admission papers of the two Dakotas and blindly signed them. Only later was it decided that North Dakota was admitted first, as the 39th state, while South Dakota became the 40th state. The order was probably determined alphabetically.

Benjamin Harrison

• Salem Sue is the world's biggest Holstein cow. A roadside animal sculpture built in 1974, the giant bovine stands 38 feet (12 m) tall and is 50 feet (15 m) long. It weighs 6 tons (5.4 metric tons). The town of New Salem is in south-central North Dakota, close to Interstate I-94. From the roadway, people can spot Salem Sue for miles around. It peers down from a hillside northwest of the town. The statue was built to promote the area's dairy industry.

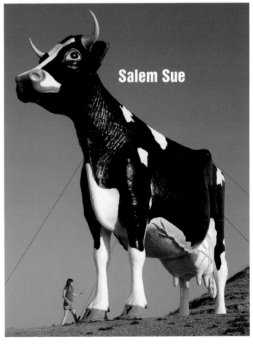
Salem Sue

PEOPLE

Louis L'Amour (1908-1988) was one of the most successful writers of all time. He wrote more than 100 books and hundreds of short stories, most of which were Westerns. He remains one of the most popular authors in the world. More than 200 million copies of his books are in print. Dozens of his novels were turned into Hollywood movies. His stories featured spectacular action and plots that galloped forward at breakneck speed. His most popular novels include *Hondo* (1953), *How the West Was Won* (1963), *Flint* (1960), and *Last of the Breed* (1987). L'Amour was born in Jamestown, North Dakota.

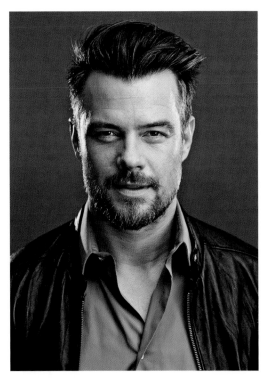

Josh Duhamel (1972-) is a popular Hollywood movie and television actor. He began his career as a model, and then moved into acting. He played Leo du Pres on the soap opera *All My Children*, which led to him winning a Daytime Emmy Award. He is most famous for his roles in the first three *Transformers* movies, and for the television show *Las Vegas*. In 2009, he married Fergie of the band The Black Eyed Peas. Duhamel was born and grew up in Minot, North Dakota.

Eric Sevareid (1912-1992) was a television journalist who worked for the CBS network. He first became famous during World War II, when he reported on the German invasion of Paris, France. In 1943, his plane was shot down over Burma (today's Myanmar). He was rescued behind enemy lines. He was a popular reporter because he helped people understand the news. Sevareid was born in Velva, North Dakota.

Dr. Anne Carlsen (1915-2002) was born without forearms or lower legs. Despite her disability, she learned to use her arm stubs to do everyday tasks like feed herself, write, and even drive a car. She earned a teaching degree in 1936. In 1938, she started work at a school for children with disabilities

in Fargo, North Dakota. The school soon moved to Jamestown, North Dakota. After earning her doctorate degree in 1949, Carlsen was named principal of the school, and then superintendent. She worked at the school for more than 40 years, helping disabled students become successful citizens. She retired in 1981, but worked as a consultant until her death. Today, the school is named the Anne Carlsen Center for Children. Dr. Carlsen was born in Wisconsin, but spent most of her adult life in North Dakota.

Phil Jackson (1945-) had one of the most successful coaching careers in the history of the National Basketball Association (NBA). He was a star high school player in Williston, North Dakota. After playing for the University of North Dakota in Grand Forks, he began his NBA career with the New York Knicks and the New York Nets. In 1989, he was named head coach of the Chicago Bulls, helping the team win six championships in nine seasons. He also coached the Los Angeles Lakers to many winning seasons. He was named NBA Coach of the Year in 1996. He retired from coaching in 2011, after winning 11 NBA championships. In 2014, he became president of the New York Knicks organization. Jackson was born in Montana, but grew up in Williston, North Dakota.

CITIES

Fargo is the biggest city in North Dakota. Its population is about 115,863. It is located along the Red River of the North in the southeastern part of the state. Fargo was founded in 1871 as a stopping point for riverboats. Today, the city is a center for North Dakota's industry, education, retail, and arts scene. The biggest employers include education, banking, insurance, construction, and health care. North Dakota State University enrolls more than 14,500 students. The Fargo Theatre is a famous restored art deco movie theater built in 1926. The Plains Art Museum is in a renovated warehouse downtown. The largest museum in the state, it features thousands of works of fine art from all over the world. The Fargo Air Museum preserves many vintage aircraft, and includes a replica of a 1903 *Wright Flyer*.

Bismarck is the capital of North Dakota. Its population is 68,896. It is located in the south-central part of the state. Founded in 1872, its original name was Edwinton. The following year, the name was changed to Bismarck, after German leader Otto von Bismarck. The city hoped to attract new German residents to the area. Today, Bismarck is a fast-growing city. It is the economic hub of central North Dakota. Major employers include health care, education, retail, and government services. The state capitol is the tallest building in the state, standing at 242 feet (74 m). There are several colleges in the city. Nearby Fort Abraham Lincoln preserves a Mandan Native American village and the United States Army post that was once the home of Lieutenant Colonel George Custer of the Army's 7th Cavalry.

The University of North Dakota in Grand Forks is the oldest university in the state.

Grand Forks is the third-largest city in North Dakota. It is located in the heart of the Red River Valley, in the northeastern part of the state. Its population is about 56,057. The city rests at the fork of the Red River of the North and the Red Lake River, which is why it is called Grand Forks. Founded in 1870, the city today has many kinds of businesses, including health care, wind turbine manufacturing, food processing, banking, and retail stores. The University of North Dakota is the oldest college in the state. Established in 1883, it enrolls about 15,000 students. Just west of the city is Grand Forks Air Force Base, which provides hundreds of civilian jobs.

NORTH DAKOTA

A full-size replica of Norway's Gol Stave Church stands in Minot, North Dakota.

Minot is North Dakota's fourth-largest city. Its population is 47,997. It is located in the north-central part of the state. The city was founded in 1886 when the Great Northern Railway laid tracks through the area. Today, the city depends on health care, retail stores, transportation, and servicing of the oil industry. Minot Air Force Base is a few miles north of the city. It is Minot's largest employer. Minot State University enrolls about 3,500 students. Minot's Norsk Hostfest is the largest Scandinavian-American festival in North America. The city's Scandinavian Heritage Park features a full-size replica of the Gol Stave Church from Gol, Norway.

TRANSPORTATION

North Dakota has 87,078 miles (140,138 km) of public roadways. About 571 miles are interstate highways. Interstate I-94 goes east and west across the lower third of the state, passing through the cities of Fargo, Jamestown, Bismarck, and Dickinson. Interstate I-29 travels north and south through the Red River Valley in the far eastern part of the state, passing through the cities of Fargo and Grand Forks. There are 4,401 road bridges in the state.

Railroads have played an important role in North Dakota's history. Since the 1870s, the state's farm products have been shipped by rail to markets in far-away states. Today, there are 8 freight railroads hauling cargo on 3,330 miles (5,359 km) of track. The most common kinds of freight include farm and food products, crude oil, coal, chemicals, plus sand and gravel.

A grain train is loaded with more than 20 million pounds (9 million kg) of spring wheat at an elevator in Sterling, North Dakota.

The Amtrak Empire Builder in Minot, North Dakota. The train runs from Chicago, Illinois, to Seattle, Washington.

Amtrak serves North Dakota with one line that runs east and west across the state. Called the Empire Builder, it carries about 155,000 passengers each year.

North Dakota has 98 public airports. The busiest include Hector International Airport in Fargo, Bismarck Municipal Airport, Minot International Airport, and Sloulin Field International Airport in Williston.

TRANSPORTATION

NATURAL
RESOURCES

About 89 percent of North Dakota is farmland, or is used for grazing cattle and sheep. That is about 39.2 million acres (15.9 million ha) of land. The state has approximately 30,000 farms. Many of them are very large. The average size is 1,307 acres (529 ha).

Wheat is North Dakota's most important farm crop. The state is second only to Kansas in the amount harvested. In fact, North Dakota harvests enough each year to make about 16 billion loaves of wheat bread.

Other crops grown by North Dakota farmers include soybeans, corn, canola, hay, barley, potatoes, sunflowers, beans, peas, flaxseed, and oats.

Cattle and sheep are important livestock products. The state is also the top honey producer in the country.

A beekeeper from Browning's Honey, a company that has been in business since the 1930s, checks a hive near Jamestown, North Dakota.

An oil pump jack, oil storage tanks, and a truck are ready for use at the Bakken oil field near Williston, North Dakota. The state's oil boom in the 2010s brought many workers to the area and helped businesses grow.

Oil was first discovered in North Dakota in 1951, near the town of Tioga. The state became a big producer of crude oil. That grew even more in the 2010s when new oil-drilling technology helped pump millions of gallons of crude oil from the Bakken oil field in northwestern North Dakota. The oil boom employed many people and helped businesses grow. Production slowed in 2016 as prices sank, due to a worldwide glut of oil. North Dakota also produces natural gas and coal.

NATURAL RESOURCES

INDUSTRY

Less than six percent of North Dakota's workforce is employed by manufacturing companies. The state is too far from major cities, and its population is low. Most factories process food grown on North Dakota's farms. Other factories make farm equipment such as tractors. Construction equipment and petroleum products are also important. Bobcat, the maker of compact construction equipment, is the state's largest manufacturer. It has been making equipment in North Dakota since 1947. Bobcat's headquarters is in Fargo.

The service industry is a large part of North Dakota's economy. Instead of making products, companies in the service industry sell services to other businesses and consumers. The industry includes businesses such as advertising, banking, financial services, health care, insurance, restaurants, retail stores, law, marketing, and tourism.

A Bobcat plant in Bismarck, North Dakota. The company's headquarters is in Fargo.

About 20 percent of North Dakotans work in government jobs. The United States military has a big presence in the state. Grand Forks Air Force Base and Minot Air Force Base employ thousands of civilians and greatly boost local businesses.

Tourism has a big impact on North Dakota's economy. About 24 million people spend $3.6 billion yearly to hunt, fish, visit historical landmarks, or simply enjoy the state's natural beauty.

A hunter and his dog head out on the North Dakota grasslands. Hunters, anglers, and outdoor lovers bring billions of tourist dollars to the state.

SPORTS

There are no professional major league sports teams in North Dakota. The Fargo-Moorhead RedHawks play for the American Association of Independent Professional Baseball (AAIPB). This entertaining independent baseball team has won five league championships.

Many North Dakotans follow the state's college sports teams. Baseball, football, and ice hockey are especially popular. The University of North Dakota, in Grand Forks, has 19 men's and women's teams. They are nicknamed "The Fighting Hawks." Their men's hockey team has won eight National Collegiate Athletic Association (NCAA) championships. North Dakota State University, in Fargo, has 14 men's and women's teams. They are known as the North Dakota State Bison, or "The Thundering Herd."

Bull riding at a
North Dakota rodeo.

Rodeos are a big part of North Dakota's Western culture, from high school and college amateur competitions to professional events. The North Dakota Roughrider Rodeo Association Finals draws a crowd of at least 10,000 rodeo fans each year to the city of Jamestown. Rodeo competitions include bronc riding, steer wrestling, tie-down and team roping, barrel racing, and bull riding.

People in North Dakota love outdoor sports, including biking, hiking, and horseback riding. Camping, fishing, and hunting trips are a family tradition among many North Dakotans.

ENTERTAINMENT

The Dakota Zoo in Bismarck is home to hundreds of animals representing 108 species. Rare animals include Bengal tigers and black-footed ferrets. Other zoos in the state include Chahinkapa Zoo in Wahpeton, Red River Zoo in Fargo, and Roosevelt Park Zoo in Minot.

There are many places to see performing arts groups in North Dakota, including the Bismarck-Mandan Symphony Orchestra and the Lisbon Opera House. The Medora Musical is performed outdoors at the Burning Hills Amphitheatre near historic Medora. Performed nightly each summer since 1965, the popular musical celebrates the life of Theodore Roosevelt during his years in North Dakota. It features musical acts, dancing, and even live horses on stage!

A performance of the Medora Musical.

Theodore Roosevelt National Park

Theodore Roosevelt National Park is located in the heart of the Badlands. It protects more than 70,000 acres (28,328 ha) of brightly colored, eroded hills and wildlife-filled valleys. At the visitor's center, history buffs can learn about President Theodore Roosevelt.

The Enchanted Highway is a 32-mile (52-km) stretch of road between the towns of Regent and Gladstone. It features giant metal sculptures of pheasants, a tin family, deer, and the world's largest grasshopper.

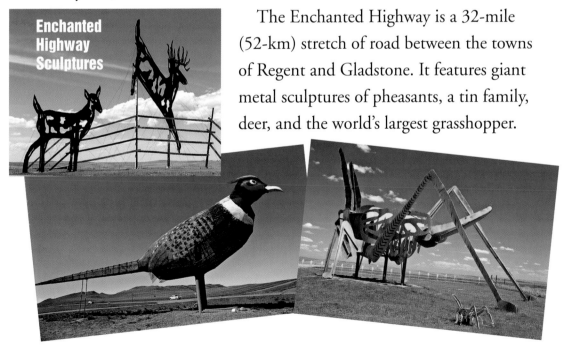

Enchanted Highway Sculptures

TIMELINE

8,000 BC—Paleo-Indians arrive in the area of present-day North Dakota. They lead a nomadic existence, hunting mammoths and bison.

1500s—Cheyenne, Mandan, and Hidatsa Native Americans settle in the area, mainly along the Missouri River. The Chippewa and Sioux live throughout the plains of eastern and central North Dakota.

1682—France claims all land around the Mississippi River, including North Dakota. The area is called French Louisiana.

1738—French explorer La Vérendrye visits Mandan villages along the Missouri River. It is the first known contact between European people and Native Americans in North Dakota.

1803—The United States buys a huge area of North America from France. The Louisiana Purchase includes much of present-day North Dakota.

1804—Lewis and Clark, with their expedition called the Corps of Discovery, enter North Dakota. They spend the winter at Fort Mandan, along the Missouri River.

1861—Dakota Territory is officially organized. More settlers begin to arrive.

1880s—Railroads built across North Dakota bring new settlers and businesses.

1889—North Dakota becomes the 39th state in the Union.

1930s—North Dakota is hit hard by the Great Depression and a long drought.

1951—Oil is discovered in western North Dakota.

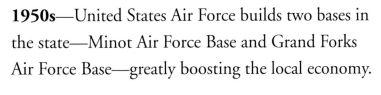

1950s—United States Air Force builds two bases in the state—Minot Air Force Base and Grand Forks Air Force Base—greatly boosting the local economy.

1978—President Carter changes North Dakota's Theodore Roosevelt National Memorial Park to Theodore Roosevelt National Park, protecting the land for all Americans.

2009—The Red River of the North floods near Fargo, North Dakota. Thousands of sandbags are placed by citizens to hold back the water.

2016—The University of North Dakota Fighting Hawks men's ice hockey team wins its eighth NCAA Men's Ice Hockey Championship.

GLOSSARY

Alberta Clipper

Quick-moving storm that bring high winds, snow, and very cold temperatures across the northern United States. These storms often begin in the western Canadian province of Alberta.

Art Deco

A type of architecture from the 1920s and 1930s. Among some people today, it is very popular as a "retro" style. Art deco uses precise, geometric shapes and bold colors.

Badlands

A desert-like area that has deep cliffs, steep rocks, and areas that have been highly eroded by water and wind.

Great Depression

A time in American history beginning in 1929 and lasting for several years when many businesses failed across the country and millions of people lost their jobs.

Great Plains

The land east of the Rocky Mountains, west of the Mississippi River and stretching from Canada to the Mexican border. It is mostly covered with grass and few trees.

Lewis and Clark Expedition

An exploration of western North America, led by Meriwether Lewis and William Clark, from 1804-1806.

Louisiana Purchase

A purchase by the United States from France in 1803 of a huge section of land west of the Mississippi River. The United States nearly doubled in size after the purchase. The young country paid about $15 million for more than 828,000 square miles (2.1 million sq km) of land. Most of North Dakota was part of the Louisiana Purchase.

Mandan

A Native American tribe that lived in present-day North Dakota before the arrival of Europeans. They lived in permanent villages along the Missouri River and two of its tributaries, the Knife and Heart Rivers.

Nomads

People who don't live in one place. Nomads are constantly traveling, usually following animal herds, which they hunt for food.

Prairie

An ecosystem that includes grasses and flowering plants. Most of the plant roots are deep under the surface. It takes many years for prairies to form. Frequent fires burn off dead material and return nutrients to the soil. Deep-rooted plants then re-sprout. This cycle of death and regrowth forms rich, black soil over many thousands of years.

Smallpox

A deadly disease brought by Europeans that wiped out many North Dakota Native American villages in the 1700s and 1800s. Native Americans had no natural immunity to the disease.

INDEX